Tributaries

Tributaries
© 2025, Aspen Everett

No part of this book may be reproduced by any means known at this time or derived henceforth without written permission of the publisher or author. The exception would be in the case of brief quotations embodied in the critical articles or reviews and pages where permission is specifically granted by the publisher or author.

Books may be purchased in quantity and/or special sales by contacting the publisher. All inquiries related to such matters should be addressed to:

Middle Creek Publishing & Audio 9161
Pueblo Mountain Park Road Beulah,
CO 81023
middlecreekpublishing@outlook.com
(719) 369-9050

First Paperback Edition, 2025
ISBN: 9781957483375

Cover Art: Image by Tree Bernstein .

Cover Design: David Anthony Martin, Middle Creek Publishing & Audio.

Tributaries

Aspen Everett

Middle Creek Publishing & Audio
Beulah, CO USA

Dedicated to the More-than-Human

and all seeking (re)connection

Table of Contents

All Water Has Perfect Memory	1
▽	
The Sediment of New Beginnings	3
Populus deltoides	5
A {Paleocene} Sea of Possibility	7
Passing through Kansas	8
Maclura pomifera – A Ghost Story	9
Harvest Season	11
▽	
Returning to Wichita	12
Geranium	14
Coyote Taught Me Poetry	16
The Cost of Living	19
The Body is a River of Breaths	21
Wild Sunflowers on a Dirt Road	23
▽	
What is the Color of Transformation?	25
Pine Trees Covered in Snow	28
The Lightning Won't Listen	29
Platanus occidentalis	31
Follow the River	32

More than Human 33
Communion 35
▽
Confluence 36

"There are no unsacred places;
there are only sacred places
and desecrated places."

Wendell Berry

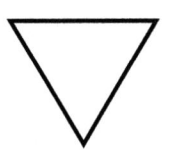

All Water Has Perfect Memory

Each little grain is me
each alluvium sand of the sea
this riverbank becoming
enormous
this tributary, this artery,
this systole and diastole
pulsing planet
feed the sea,
the heart of me
remembering

sometimes something disastrous:
an oil spill in the river
an ocean on fire
radiation
meltdown
chemicals and toxicity
what wicked runoff
plastiglomerate coagulant

give me a flood
a sudden cleansing
washing
away
the levee

sand of the sea, body of me
salt of my tears
the taste of lost futures
the waters remind me
of wholeness

the sand, it sticks to the skin
every grain of this earth body
becoming

rise
the rivers rising
take me
take me
rushing waters

*"Because even a river can be lonely,
even a river will die of thirst."*
Natalie Diaz

The Sediment of New Beginnings

I exist within the eternities of earth and sky.
I exist within you, coursing through
every cell of your being. I am you.
You beckon me from heaven to be
culled in cold cloud comfort
until I am weighted with longing
and fall upon mountains.
Sunshine and gravity coax me
from sleep and I runoff the mountaintop,
creating the timeless histories of stone and sea.
I have given shape to the land and eventually
all mountains bow to me.
I will carry the sediment of new beginnings.
My banks beget mountains again and again
on my journey to you.
You, all life, I sustain.
Kneel on my banks and part your parched lips.
Drink deep.
We exist as one.
You bleed the Mother's milk
that I have wept for you.
I knew you within the womb,
afloat in amniotic fluid.
You traded gills for lungs and grew feet
to walk upon the land
and hands to build factories and pipelines
to pollute me with your ignorance and greed.
Can you not see that
what you do to me you do to yourselves?

Dams cannot withhold my fury.
I am on a journey
into the oceans of eternity.
I've got to go, got to go, got to flow,
sky is calling me home, but
I will return riding the wheel of life.
Pray that I no longer contain your venom.
Acid rain withers the crops
I have long sustained.
Remember that I belong not to you alone,
but all life.
I am within the very cells of all your relations.
I am soul.
I am spirit.
Will your soul need Brita filtration?
Make me clean. Allow me to be.
I must continue to reach the sea
so that I may return to the sky
to nourish the earth below and quench your thirst
so that we can be together in our longing.
I am Water and I am you.

Mni Wiconi!

Populus deltoides

O' Cottonwood,
sing to me of bottomlands and rivers,
wetlands, and tinctures
to heal the wounds of too few
forgotten forests felled
beneath till and plow
such softness
such growth
keeper of the canopy
reseeding
tufts on the water
such brittle mother
short lived
giving limbs to the wind
dancing with gravity
toppled in the rush of weather
reaching into the infinite blue
the sensation of worlds inverted
an intonation of time and
I am beneath oceans
the movements of wind like water
I am electric
waiting for the lightning
my darling
bane of man-agement
in falling, a habitat

rivers held in her arms
stilled in their rushing and
fish find rest in the shade of filtered pools
while birds alight the hollows and
barred owl leaves sign of her passing
deer wander, unabated by asphalt
and poets remember to listen
to breathe in the vanilla of resin
to break before bending
what lesson in falling
for now, towering
chlorophyll dreams awakening
the soft down of summer
beginning

A {Paleocene} Sea of Possibility

When life snakes
and winds as the limbs of an Osage,
which thin brittle branch shall support
the weight of unknowing?
Will roots pleat deep the dry soil of home,
this word as elusive as sky to leaf,
or will life grow heavy in gravity
of falling fruit that no mouth will eat?
    Am i to be Cottonwood,
        scattered on the wind?
The riverbends of germination never really end,
    for there is, as Patti Smith sings,
        "a Sea of Possibility."
Do horses hide in my blonde waves?
Will i find the spine to ride one outta here alive
    or be trampled by the sharp hooves of
        doubt and deliberation?
Osage tears itself apart in time.
Gnarled young begotten by roots,
forever searching.

Passing through Kansas

A journey into Underlands,
down back roads.
All the pressure of the bottom of the ocean.
Did I drink from the river of forgotten?
Closed store fronts,
no groceries nor library or school.
Old men hold to what they own,
conservative as cotton.
The topsoil gives to the wind,
and the rains, when they come,
overflow a river of woe.
The ghosts, you can hear them,
by the side of the road.

Maclura pomifera – A Ghost Story

Osage anachronism\this love affair with phantoms
this once savannah\these haunted grasslands
Where are you my mastodon, my mammoth?

grazing ghosts\eat of my allure
this strange fruit\falling\an offering
to you\my seed\seeking shadows
to spread\ this offering\ rottening

I am the evolution of ancestors without future\
forgotten seven sisters\mere megafauna memory\
my limbs reaching\twisted trunks gaping\
my twisted figure answering

I am a living monument to loss\a growing gravestone\
haunted by extinction\out of time\this Pleistocene
repeating\epoch of exorcism\Anthropocene blues\
this fragmented song\so many missing singers\
the gatherers forced elsewhere\Kansas bereft of the tribe
from whom it stole its title\hunter and hunted\cut
from me\bow of Osage\sinew string\these lands\
dressed in genocide\ in buffalo robes\ a tower of skulls

haunted by oceans\all the pressure and silence\
all the noise and violence\ waves crashing\ land
of limestone\karstic country\rivers of forgetting\
ancient organic matter\man-manipulated

-a cremation millions of years in the making-

combustion engine\petroleum byproducts\becoming
gasoline\becoming oil\becoming pipeline\becoming
polluted waters\becoming lost futures\becoming
coal\becoming capital\becoming carbon emission\

becoming hole in the ozone\becoming fire in the ocean\becoming ghost\becoming lost\becoming haunting\\becoming burning\\

-the past fed to the fires of insatiable future-

monstrous appetite\over consumption\man hunts megafauna to extinction\accelerates loss\ ignores anachronisms\ we trees\ mourning\ this hedgerow\ this division\ this fragmentation

haunted ecos\man as maker of ghosts

Harvest Season

poor little fledgling thought hidden,
      unable yet to fly

the Combines are coming
to raze the field

discarded,   half selves
dry   barren earth   sharp to heel
invasive   grass returns, even slowly
choking what is   what was   what should be
fenced fields meticulously mown:
careful attention to cubic yield
flightless roots   but not too deep
eroding topsoil - collapse of culture
the farmer even   fed to profit
combine capital decapitating   family
for to feed is not enough
trademark seed - patent product
plants monetized   cash seed only
no growth but in shares
share: a strange word   misplaced, maybe?
to share the products of the sun, of water and soil,
toil, labor, sweat,   earth eating bodies and
mosquitoes well-fed, skin cancer copper tones & red
neck bent over loans & disaster
this nature: hail & thunderstorms,
bugs & pests, blight & nitrogen ratio, salted
soil, fertilized   minds, like small birds
      unable yet to fly

The Combines, they do not stop
cannot stop

"Bury me not on the lone prairie…"

Returning to Wichita

and the expanse opened before me
       mountains   receding
consuming sky,   blue hunger,
      cloudless teeth
into the land of hungry
coming down from the high country

the further from Denver the more the road   cracks
               and breaks apart
loud highway hum,   rubber tire lullaby
overheating engine, gears grinding,   wear &
tear of distant horizons
an endless sea   of thirst
      wind turbines forever turning   slowly

drifting   was i asleep?

     and having been swallowed whole
       into the grotesque throat
what happens when within the belly of a whale
small bonfires burn like beaches?
will it spit you back into cool blue?

the immensity of blue –
     too much to swallow,   to drink
the crushing sky, the pulverizing calm
       of receding waters
blue stones,   sand-kissed around Her wrist
Her blue eyes, your blue songs,

        sung from blue lips

what songs will you sing at your funeral?
will they come from the throat?
will they sing of grotesquity, the stain of a city
      you can't run away from?

abandoned buildings like teeth
      all broken windows

streetlamps
      and there's that hum again

the highway beckons

Geranium

a blackbird flies backwards from tinted window
and you are caught in its starling shadow
waking cracks climbing the sides of
these feeble buildings

the buildings are in a perpetual state of falling
only grey skies hold them in place

the grey tone of your voice contemplates weather
as if that were the only geranium
your throat could grow

it is better to speak in chrysanthemums,
lupine, perhaps shooting star

this city led you, little antelope,
into a cunning enclosure

you never learned how to jump,
never learned Indian Paintbrush
but you know how to run

wide open calls you home
in a language of blue
blue that holds your heart in place,
keeps it from killing you

your pillow was covered
in blackbird feathers
if only it were a sign

winged thing sits on your chest
in the night to cry, but not in words

paved over rivers can still drown deer brothers
and sisters, if only this were fable

then struggle would be no more than lesson
transformation wouldn't be so fatal
curses could be lifted with the correct incantations

you are hooves and ochre, sawdust and iron
blessed by coarse calico, be they ropes or binding

this city called to you three times and
three times you answered with lips like milkweed

your geraniums are malnourished monotone grey
where is the wild thing you once knew?
was domestic chosen for you?

remember to run when the wind calls
remember the buildings will fall
do not let them take you when they topple

you are so much more than this Underland and ash
you are flowers and flight
you are the generation of beginning

plant your seeds in the mouths of everyone you meet
may it be brighter when they speak
to sew gardens over civilizations

a place without shadows or fences
where antelope run
and run, and run

Coyote Taught Me Poetry

Where I'm from,
wind was a ceaseless baptism,
tall grass was once an ocean,
Bison were once a keystone species.

I am from the Underland —
fenced fields upon fields of Asphodel
        and muddy rivers.
           Ninnescah named me.

Iron tracks crisscross the landscape of my chest.
Redtail taught me to see,   Redwing to sing,
      both to believe in wings from wounds.

The horizon was a window into tomorrow.
Yesterday   was a rising sun;
        magenta/marigold/mango;
a painting painted in katabatic wind.

The flatland was a window into all your secrets.
Everyone could always see what you were doing,
      where you were going   —
          there was nowhere to go.

We drove in circles, guzzling gasoline / ethanol,
        PBR, packs n' packs of Marlboro.

There was a christ on every corner, but
there was no food that could feed you,
only drive-thru dollar menus, Narcan, herbicide,
      white bread;
only tap-water that would set itself on fire.

We were bonfires.
    We lit up the country,
      drove too fast down gravel roads.

We were rollovers and beauty queens
    killed on 4wheelers,
      killed by teenage pregnancy.

There must be something in the water,
something in the boredom that killed us
    until we killed ourselves
    with fentanyl and car collisions,

something to the unbearable weight of ancient
oceans collapsing above our heads
like pressure building
    when god's always watching.

We were spoon-fed so many holy ghosts.
Our tables were set with slaughter and monoculture.
    We prayed, and were preyed upon.

We drank cough syrup to forget our crucifixions,
huffed whip-its until we couldn't hear the angels
with all that pounding in our temples; swallowed
thunderheads and tornadoes by the mouthful.

    I was breastfed on lightning,
      nursed by a lonely prairie,
      and all her polluted tributaries.

Like Coyote,
I was always hungry.

envoi

My body is a land of limestone,
       karstic, hollow, just as malleable,
       a living structure where the dead
       carve their initials.

The Cost of Living

The Owl high in the hedgerow reeks of death.

A trick of paradise prairie –
rural living   cheap rent   my beautiful exile
     growing weaker
     an attack of phantoms
     no one knows what's wrong
abdominal monsters hiding beneath
amber oceans of uncut wheat,
fields of bright green bovine bounty
     soybean genetically patented
     fattened cattle   out to pasture
     only the ghost of antelope

Dead canaries in the milo
septic well water ratio – we drilled too deep,
too close to what we excrete
     grey water runoff   a white vapor fog
anhydrous ammonia prayers preying on
tilled and re-tilled decarbonized depleted fields
     miracle growth
the annual anxiety of growing
     profit margins
the nightmare of monoculture monopoly

forty acres of fenced in freedom:
my sanctuary, my solitude, my silence,
my strychnine baited trap
cancer in clover   the luxury of bare feet

        unmown grass   agrarian wild child
headaches,   dizziness   losing focus, and memory
      doubled over
          what can i eat?
          poison tastes like food

The Great Horned Owl watches me.
My proximity sends it silently into the coming dusk.
Its talons are starlight sharp,
          ready for the kill.

Do we agree to our death sentence,
as the field mouse makes treaty with the Owl,
accepting without question
the terms and conditions of a lease?

my signature, my debt
it cost more than i could know

The Body is a River of Breaths

i lay listening to my heart beat beneath its ribcage
from a hospital bed i never thought i'd be in
        the pain, the poison
                this inflammation
                this myopericarditis

there must be a rhythm to my arrhythmia
all electric — i am disconnected
learning the lesson of broken

what does it mean to swell,
to be constricted,
to swallow prescriptions given
to fight this affliction
        this novel virus

i can feel the blood moving,
the oceans beneath my skin
veins like estuaries

the body is a river of breaths,
a moving migration of matter

an infection
like oil spilled in the river
        a dam
        an expansion
what the heart can't take
        this release

this giving vial after vial
        IVs and oil wells
the calamity of immobile
the heart is constricted but

the body is a confluence of capillaries
         and coastal rivers teeming
with slick salmon at long last
returning to the mouth of the spill
where whales congregate
        and sing
unimpeded by blockage
        or swell
to sink ships
        like white bloods cells

those rivers, these tributaries
        like arteries
of the living breathing mother body

sandhill cranes take to wing
        like wind from these lungs
a riparian oscillation of a thousand
           beating wings

sometimes as slowly as monarch migrations
        generations in the making
or pulsing like a bloodstream of somatic salmon
        exhaling oceans

their deaths but diadromous breaths
feeding the beating heart of cedar haunted forests

feeding grizzly, feeding osprey, wolves returning
becoming trophic cascade becoming waterfall
becoming stream becoming buffalo
drinking from a glassy lake
becoming me
sleeping beneath a saline sea
wired to this great Gaia teaching me
the EKG of a planet alive and whispering
      -the blood is me-
       and drink
from the sea of becoming
the lessons of the heart are just beginning

Wild Sunflowers on a Dirt Road

Wilderness was a riparian road leading home.
      Yes,   a road.
A man-made artifice,   a scar,
deeper than the ones in my arm.

Wilderness was neither destination nor sycamore.
Wilderness was walking away from time & obligation,
to sit with the eternity of flowers & rivers.
What have I to offer coralline clouds but longing?

Rainstorms and rivers —
wilderness was the land of baptism & promise,
that all things would be green or golden,
      sunflowers or ocean.

Wilderness was a sanctuary of egrets & herons.
From desecration,   belonging.

Ninnescah is a word that flows
      from the river of my mouth.

Though it was not made for my tongue,
      I am made of its mud.

In a world of scars and artifacts,
      what can we belong to?

The flowers belong to the sand, the shore,
      the sediment,
            while I am mostly erosion.

Animal body, corrosive   carnivore.
Have I come to consume the sunflower
      seed to feed only myopic me?

Remember reciprocity, scars & forgiven.
I am the road & the river,
        the storm,   & the flower.
            The roots,
                        like roads,
how deep
do they go?

*"For the soul is wanderer
with many hands and feet."*
Joy Harjo

What is the color of transformation?

is it   red   orange
Adonis flowers and flames
fire licked forests forcing creatures from comforts
heat unyielding, hot-tempered   anger
danger / destruction   becoming creation
Indian paintbrush,   wild strawberries,
raspberries with many little seeds and healing
leaves changing seasons
rose hips alongside red deer trails
leading little red cap towards
pomegranate promises and amanita dreams
of tangerine sunrise wounding

azure skies
       endless expanse   daunting
turquoise west stones following
ice-blue glacier rivers shifting descent
becoming coastal waters caressing continents
       unknown depths

of cerulean eyes finding
magpie feathers gathered
little charms adorning altars alongside
rose quartz and amethyst
the color of intuition transforming
purple bruising into lilac cut
dusk flaunting magenta wrinkles
painted with maroon wild plums and
lavender healing oils

is transformation painted in primrose?
so many colors carefully cultivated
like marigold hair laughing with
Arnica wild wind
as dawn becomes day   again
little flecks of morning caught in her amber
    eyes golden and green
witnessing the alchemy
of shifting landscapes
    wheat fields,   golden to ochre
a yellow line divides gilded corn
on either side
    baled hay   wet alfalfa
the coming harvest,
feasting and merriment
    sun-kissed honey wine
transmuting minds smiling

what is the color of laughter?
the sudden opening of sunflowers
Meadowlark singing
dandelion's promise of summer before
leaving us to the wind

scattered seeds
white as snow
forms disappear beneath
the equality of cold
anything is possible
all colors and none

maybe transformation is green seeds germinating
        beneath a canvas of white?
barren hillsides transfigured before the eyes
into chlorophyll color of life –
        virid grasses, lamb's ear,
          milkweed, mullein, mint
the emerald green of yarrow leaves
a poultice for the pain of metamorphosis
Aspen groves pleating beneath while
above little buds beget bright charms
dancing woodlands and shadows
celadon waters and verdant wet moss
rolling hills folded into horizons like
many Celtic knots

silver polished
        mercurial moon
        Loba on all fours
she wears a kaleidoscope of colors in her fur

is transformation   Bifrost binding
beginnings and ends
        yesterday-today-tomorrow
chrysalis perception of possibility
and butterfly dreams
ruminating lightwaves at last piercing
the multicolored lining of your cocoon opening
to painted prism wings wearing
every bend in the rainbow

What comes next when ready to fly?

Pine Trees Covered in Snow

pine boughs bend easily
beneath the weight of water
towards release
while steadfast to wild winds
letting a little light in
only when it is time to fall

in falling,   an opening

The Lightning Won't Listen

i write with fever   ignited by lightning
too long dancing in the cold Beltane rain
wetting the wanting earth   shimmering
and green   beneath my bare feet
clothing cast aside for vulnerability

i am a lightning rod looking for connection
of hot heavenly bodies –

         strike me
with lightning-like love,
              electric intimacy

i am tree-like, with roots pleating
     an inverted imitation
and trees, for their part, reaching
  - limbs like openings

saying,
    yes
    I would hold you

twisted and charred
split by a sky kiss and the closing distance
i have seen these sky trees split open
        in their wanting

does the lightning curse its impermanence?
        a fleeting flirtation

my nervous system attempting
flattery through imitation
synopsis connection - revelation of
one-hundred and three degrees:

      all is seeking connection
      a journey   towards wholeness

the applause of thunder
hail to the halleluiah miraculous meeting
of storm fronts and wind currents
      booming love

i desire
to taste lightning on my lips
blood battles rain
coursing through every membrane
wanting connection

i'm howling with the wind
arms like branches
but the lightning won't listen

the storm passes
and i shiver

Platanus occidentalis

O' Sycamore
hold me gently, mother night
your skin,   so like mine
let me lay my hand on the fabled folds of cambium
you,   so exposed
discarding your woodland robe
      unneeded rhytidome
she lets them in,   holds them
the owl, the mouse,   woodpecker and wren,
chittering den of squirrels hidden in her hollows
how does she hold herself so high
      like lightning, reaching
        impermanence, planted
a reflection of heavens
keeper of rivers
she breathes the poison of me
      takes it
apothecary
lightning white sign of water

i dreamed she presented me with a simple fig
so many little seeds, like grains of sand
an hourglass upturned
      my time on this earth
      at an end
i ate them all,
food for the journey
i will not be returning
and she shall be the last thing i see
      my coffin lid   closing

O' Sycamore,   O' Mother Night
hold me

Follow the River

to find what is left of the wildlands

follow the dirt road that ends at the river

cross the iron tracks

do not look back

turn at the twisted Osage

around the Beaver-made lake

the Deer know the way

ignore the no trespassing warnings

read the otherside,

blissfully blank

silent Bobcat speaks in paw prints

mating Redtails cry welcome

those that have come before have painted

cathedrals of abandon

follow the river

beyond the rattle-clack of boxcar

gather some bones

sit in the sun

there are many paths to take

all of them will help you

lose your way

More than Human

I am the body, bone, blood of ecology.
I am the stone, the sea, sediment and sinew.
I am the deer, the elk, the antelope,
the iron, veins of silver, the ripples atop
glassy water, the salted shoreline in winter.

I am in possession of *Being* –
being human,   for now.
Being mycelium treaty with carbon,
a tree in the making,
a crane dancing.

I am the coal, the petroleum,
the ancient dead ocean floor,
the wheat, the sunlight transformed.
I am stardust and space rocks,
the violence of gravity,
landslides and wildfire.
I read the biology of me,
a landscape, like a story.
Into this inevitability I go,
a returning, a Re-membering of *Being*.

Rivers within me,
rivers at my feet.
I'm wading into the waters of me,
muddied in misunderstanding,
taken for granted,
the body is mostly water.
Do I bend for a drink?
Rivers, from *rivalry*,
the illusion of separation -
a capitalist misconception.

What is waste? What is want?
Can blood filter cancer from the river?
Can these tulips still kiss under an acid rain?
Heartbeat arrythmia, plastic patents,
genotoxic invader,   manipulated
cells of ourselves, older than we remember.

We clear-cut language, pulverize poems,
tear into the veins of our lungs,
dam our blood,
silence the epiphanies of chickadees.

I am the fox concealed
in the farmer's firelit field.
I am the match, the grass, the smoke and the ash.

Ecology, from *Oikos*, meaning *home*.
I am home to myself,
home to the world, home to the poem
translating for those who do not speak in sentences.
It is my job to listen and read what goes unspoken.

Ideas like organisms,
language a living thing,
growing inside you, inside me, inside *We*.

I am the revolution against the sovereign self,
this, "man above all else."
Free me from the incarceration of individuality,
a Re-Evolution of ecological *Being*.

We are but breathing bodies of Water
holding one another.

Communion

This is my body
which is given to you
the water, the erosion
the ocean, in wind
she holds you
whispers wisdom
forgotten
eat into me
banks beget mountains
roots, upended
what can we hold on to?
the impermanence
of trees
when the waters come
rushing
the violence
of nourishing
the body is a shifting story
like an hourglass
sand, given to gravity
a body,
given

*"i'm only going over that river
i'm only going over home"*

Confluence

[imagine the italics as music]

Come down, come down,   down in the river to pray
Come down, let's go down,   down in the river to pray

I am no preacher's son
I am Sigfried and hammer
I've tasted the dragon's blood
now I know we are one
I kneel on the banks and pray
to the kingdom of creation
may she take me into her flood,
take this poison from my blood

So I went down,
went down
down in the river to pray
I tried,   Lord, I tried
but the waters wouldn't let me come in
ain't no water in this world,   in this world
turn me back into an innocent man

And from the dragon's blood were
birthed several wings of rivers — diverging
each believed it to be the only stream
          the only tributary
as if our wings did not hold up the world
as if gospels were not pillars to our prayers
as if the rain were not resurrection

if it keeps on rainin'   levee's gonna break
if it keeps on rainin'   levee's gonna break
When the levee breaks,   we'll have no place to stay

Toni Morrison once said,
"All water has perfect memory
and is forever trying
to get back to where it once was."

Cryin' won't help you,
Prayin' won't do you no good
No, Cryin' won't help you,
Prayin' won't do you no good

feed the sea, the heart of me
washing away what's left of the levee
take me, take me
rushing waters
a journey into the oceans of eternity

take me to your river,
    I wanna go

make me clean,
oh, make me clean
a sea of possibility
emerging from the rivers of forgetting

take me to your river,
    I wanna know

I know a land of hunger,   of thirst
with too much to swallow,   to drink
listening to the heartbeat
the oceans beneath my skin
the confluence of capillaries and tributaries
becoming coastal waters caressing your continents
unknown depths   of heavens spilling over

and the river run wild,
the river run free
the river inside,
inside of me

a river runs through the middle of my body
only an illusion of separation
we are but breathing bodies of water
giving one to the other
and when the waters come rushing
wash me in the waters of rejuvenation and healing
     singing,   singing —

Come down, come down, down in the river to pray
come down, let's come down, down in the river to pray

in each of these songs,
        god is in the water
but I want to take god from the water
to know Her as I drink Her
to know that I am a confluence of something greater
capable of clean waters
if only I remember to lift my voice
     in reverence

so take me,
take me to your river
      I wanna go
take me to your river
      I wanna know

take me to the waters
to release my longing for a new beginning
water has always been about baptism,
      a blessing
sing with me these songs of creation
of letting go the world of old
we once called our own
let us come together as a new river
let our river be a road
            leading home

the river run wild,
the river run free,
the river inside,
inside of me
the river run slow,
the river run sweet,
the river inside,
inside of me

'An it harm none'

Let it BE

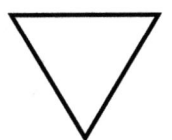

Notes & Acknowledgements

These poems were written on the traditional and unceded territories of the Kiowa, Oceti Šakowiŋ, Ute, Pawnee, Kaw/Kansa, Osage, Commanche, Apache, Wichita, Cheyenne, Arapaho, and Shoshone Nations. I extend my respects and gratitude to the many indigenous peoples who still reside here and call these lands home.

****

The title of the poem, "All Water Has Perfect Memory," is taken from a quote by Toni Morrison in reference to the habitual and historic flooding of the Mississippi River.

"The Sediment of New Beginnings" was the recipient of the 2017 Liz Caile Express Your Peace Award and would not have come to be without my involvement in the DAPL Standing Rock Protest through Mountain Forum for Peace.

"*Maclura pomifera* – A Ghost Story" was written to accompany a visual art instillation I created for the show, *Lost Futures*, which featured at Studio School in Wichita, KS in 2023.

"Geranium" was inspired by the book, *The Antelope Wife* by Louise Erdrich, and the Grimm's Fairy Tale, "Deer Brother."

"Coyote Taught Me Poetry" was written in conjunction with *A Lesson in Geopoetics*, a workshop I offered at The Firehouse Art Center in Longmont, CO in 2024. This poem, as well as "Passing through Kansas" and "Geranium," uses the term "Underland," a phrase taken from the Robert Macfarlane book of the same title.

"The Body is a River of Breaths" was inspired by the podcast episode "Terminal," produced by *Future Ecologies*, and by the essay *Creaturely Migrations on a Breathing Planet* by David Abram.

"Harvest Season" and "The Cost of Living" previously appeared in the anthology, *A Village with a Poem* (2025, Poets Choice)

"Confluence" borrows lyrics from various songs/artists including: "Down in the River to Pray," a traditional American folk-hymn popularized by Alison Krauss, "Down to the River" written by Dave Lamb, "When the Levee Breaks," written by Minnie and Joe McCoy, "River," written by Leon Bridges, and "The River Inside of Me," written by KJ Song. The line, "*let our river be a road,*" is an allusion to the song, "Rivers and Roads" by The Head and the Heart. The poem also uses the line, "*a river runs through the middle of my body,*" which is taken from the poem, "The First Water is the Body" by Natalie Diaz.

Wild Sunflowers on a Dirt Road and *Follow the River* are published online in Planted Journal (2025).

About the Author

Aspen Everett is a poet and creative from the wind-tossed flatlands of Southeast Kansas. Writing what they call *Heathen Mythology*, Aspen aims to rewrite the cultural myths of dominion and return readers to reverence for the More-than-Human. Following fetid rivers upstream until the waters ran clean, they find themselves in Boulder Colorado, beneath the shadow of Mt. Arapaho.

Tributaries is their first book.

About the Press

Middle Creek Publishing & Audio is a company seeking to make the world a better place. We are publishers of quality literature in any genre from authors and artists, both seasoned and those who are undiscovered or under-valued, or traditionally under-represented, with a great interest in works which illuminate or embody any aspect of contemplative Human Ecology, defined as the relationship between humans and their natural, social, and built environments.

Middle Creek Publishing & Audio's particular interest in Human Ecology is meant to clarify an aspect of the quality in the works we will consider for publication and as a guide to those considering submitting work to us. Our interest is in publishing works which illuminate the human experience through words, story or other *content that connects us to each other, our environment, our history, and our potential deeply and more consciously*.

In 2025, we created a nonprofit, Middle Creek Press, an NTEE A33: Arts, Culture, and Humanities - Printing and Publishing nonprofit organization. We are in the process of transitioning all work and processes over. This change will empower us to focus more on the quality of our work and extend our literary reach. Be part of this transformative journey by supporting our fundraising efforts. Any contribution helps.

www.ingramcontent.com/pod-product-compliance
Lightning Source LLC
Chambersburg PA
CBHW062121080426
42734CB00012B/2943